THE SECRET OF THE GOLDEN FLOWER

THE SECRET OF THE

GOLDEN FLOWER

[T'AI I CHIN HUA TSUNG CHIH]

BY WANG CHONGYANG

*TRANSLATED BY RICHARD WILHELM;
TRANSLATED FROM GERMAN BY CARY
F. BAYNES*

ISBN: 978-1-957990-12-5
Published by Ancient Wisdom Publication
http://www.bigfontbooks.com

Contents

Introduction

The Secret of the Golden Flower ("Tai Yi Jin Hua Zong Zhi"), a Chinese Taoist book about meditation, was translated by Richard Wilhelm (also translator, in the 1920s, of the Chinese philosophical classic the I Ching). Wilhelm, a friend of Carl Jung, was German, and his translations from Chinese to German were later translated to English by Cary F. Baynes. According to Wilhelm, Lü Dongbin was the main originator of the material presented in the book (a section below, Reception from Chinese Taoists, suggests that the material is from Quanzhen School founder Wang Chongyang, a student of Lü Dongbin.) More recently (1991), the same work has been translated by Thomas Cleary, a scholar of Eastern studies.

Despite the varieties of impressions, interpretation and opinion expressed by Wilhelm, Jung and Cleary, the meditation technique described by The Secret of the Golden Flower is a straightforward, silent method; the book's description of meditation has been characterized as 'Zen with details'. The meditation technique, set forth in poetic language, reduces to a formula of sitting, breathing and contemplating.

Sitting primarily relates to a straight posture. Breathing is described in detail, primarily in terms of the esoteric physiology of the path of qi (also known as chi or ki), or breath energy. The energy path associated with breathing has been described as similar to an internal wheel vertically aligned with the spine. When breathing is steady, the wheel turns forward, with breath energy rising in back and descending in front. Bad breathing habits (or bad posture, or even bad thoughts) may cause the wheel not to turn, or move backward, inhibiting the circulation of essential breath energy. In contemplation, one watches thoughts as they arise and recede.

The meditation technique is supplemented by descriptions of affirmations of progress in the course of a daily practice, suggesting stages that could be reached and phenomenon that may be observed such as a feeling of lightness, like floating upward or slight levitation. Such benefits are ascribed to improved internal energy associated with breath energy circulation, improvements that alleviate previously existing impediments. Several drawings portray imagery relevant to the personal evolution of a meditation practitioner, images that may be somewhat confusing in terms of pure rational analysis. "Only after one hundred days of consistent work, only then is the light genuine; only then can one begin to work with the spirit-fire."

The first such illustration represents the first one hundred days, or gathering the light. The second one represents an emergence of meditative consciousness. The third stage represents a meditative awareness that exists even in mundane, daily life. Stage 4 represents a higher meditative perception, where all conditions are recognized. Then, varied conditions are portrayed as separately perceived, yet each separate perception is part of a whole of awareness.

Heavenly Consciousness
(The Heart)

Master Lu-tsu said, That which exists through itself is called the Way (Tao). Tao has neither name nor shape. It is the one essence [Hsing], the one primal spirit. Essence and life cannot be seen. They are contained in the light of heaven. The light of heaven cannot be seen. It is contained in the two eyes. Today I will be your guide and will first reveal to you the secret of the Golden Flower of the great One, and starting from that, I will explain the rest in detail.

The great One is the term given to that which has nothing above it. The secret of the magic of life consists in using action in order to attain non-action. One must not wish to leap over everything and penetrate directly. The maxim handed down to us is to take in hand the work on human nature (hsing). In doing this is important not to take any wrong path.

The Golden Flower is the light. What color is the light? One uses the Golden Flower as a symbol. It is the true energy of the translucent great one. The phrase "The lead of the water-region has but one taste" refers to it.

[*** Heaven created water through the One (Hsing). That is the true energy of the Great One. If man attains this One he becomes alive; if he loses it he dies. But even if man lives in the energy (vital breath, prana) he does not see the energy (prana), just as fishes live in water but do not see the water. Man dies when he has no vital breath, just as fishes perish when deprived of water. Therefore the adepts have taught people to holdfast to the primal, and to guard the One; it is the circulation of the light and the maintaining of the center. If one guards this true energy, one can prolong the span of life, and can then apply the method of creating an immortal body by "melting and mixing".]

The work on the circulation of the light depends entirely on the backward-flowing movement, so that the thoughts (the place of heavenly consciousness, the heavenly heart) are gathered together. The heavenly heart lies between sun and moon (the two eyes).

The Book of the Yellow Castle says: "In the square inch field of the square foot house, life can be regulated". The square foot house is the face. The square inch field in the face:

what could that be other than the heavenly heart? In the middle of the square inch dwells the splendour. In the purple hall of the city of jade dwells the God of Utmost Emptiness and Life. The Confucians call it the center of emptiness; the Buddhist, the terrace of living; the Taoists, the ancestral land, or the yellow castle, or the dark pass, or the space of former heaven. The heavenly heart is like the dwelling place, the light is the master.

Therefore when the light circulates, the energies of the whole body appear before its throne, as, when a holy king has established the capital and has laid down the fundamental rules of order, all the states approach with tribute; or as, when the master is quiet and calm, men-servants and maids obey his orders of their own accord, and each does his work.

Therefore you have only to make the light circulate: that is the deepest and most wonderful secret. The light is easy to move, but difficult to fix. If it is made to circulate long enough, then it crystallizes itself; that is the natural spirit-body. This crystallized spirit is formed beyond the nine heavens. It is the condition of which it is said in the Book of the Seal of the Heart: "Silently thou fliest upward in the morning".

In carrying out this fundamental principle you need to seek for no other methods, but must only concentrate your thoughts on it. The book Leng Yen says: "By collecting the thoughts one can fly and will be born in heaven". Heaven is not the wide blue sky but the place where corporeality is begotten in the house of the Creative. If one keeps this up for a long time there develops quite naturally, in addition to the body, yet another spirit-body.

The Golden Flower is the Elixir of Life (Chin-tan, golden pill). All changes of spiritual consciousness depend upon the heart. There is a secret charm which, although it works very accurately, is yet so fluid that it needs extreme intelligence and clarity, and the most complete absorption and tranquility. People without this highest degree of intelligence and understanding do not find this highest degree of intelligence and understanding do not find the way to apply the charm; people without this utmost capacity for absorption and tranquility cannot keep fast hold of it.

[*** This section explains the origin of the great Way (the Tao) of the world. The heavenly heart is the germ of the great Way. If you can be absolutely quiet then the heavenly heart will spontaneously manifest itself. When the feeling stirs and expresses itself in the normal flow, man is created as primal creature. This creature abides between conception and birth in true space; when the one note of individuation enters into the birth, human nature and life are divided in two. From this time on, if the utmost quietness is not achieved, human nature and life never see each other again.

Therefore it is said in The Plan of the Supreme Ultimate that the great One includes within itself true energy (prana), seed, spirit, animus and anima. If the thoughts are absolutely tranquil so that the heavenly heart can be seem, the spiritual intelligence reaches the origin unaided. This human nature lives indeed in true space, but the radiance of the light dwells in the two eyes. Therefore the Master teaches the circulation of the light so that the true human nature may be reached. The true human nature is the primal spirit. The primal spirit is precisely human nature and life, and if one accepts what is real in it, it is the primal energy. And the great Way is just this thing.

The Master is further concerned that people should not miss the way that leads from conscious action to unconscious non-action. Therefore he says, the magic of the Elixir of Life makes use of conscious action in order that unconscious non-action may be attained. Conscious action consists in setting the light in circulation by reflection in order to make manifest the release of heaven, If then the true seed is born, and the right method applied in order to melt and mix it, and in that way to create the Elixir of Life, then one goes through the pass. The embryo, which must be developed by the work of warming, nourishing, bathing, and washing, is formed. That passes over into the realm of unconscious non-action. A whole year of this fire-period is needed before the embryo is born, sheds the shells, and passes out of the ordinary world into the holy world.

This method is quite simple and easy. But there are so many transforming and changing conditions connected with it that it is said that not with one leap can a man suddenly get there. Whoever seeks eternal life must search for the place whence human nature and life originally sprang.]

The Primal Spirit and the Conscious Spirit

Master Lu-tsu said, "In comparison with heaven and earth, man is like a mayfly. But compared to the great Way, heaven and earth, too, are like a bubble and a shadow. Only the primal spirit and the true nature overcome time and space".

The energy of the seed, like heaven and earth, is transitory, but the primal spirit is beyond the polar differences. Here is the place whence heaven and earth derive their being. When students understand how to grasp the primal spirit they overcome the polar opposites of light and darkness and tarry no longer in the three worlds. But only he who has envisioned human nature's original face is able to do this.

When men are set free from the womb, the primal spirit dwells in the square inch (between the eyes), but the conscious spirit dwells below in the heart. This lower fleshly heart has the shape of a large peach: it is covered by the wings of the lungs, supported

by the liver, and served by the bowels. This
heart is dependent on the outside world. If
a man does not eat for one day even, it feels
extremely uncomfortable. If it hears something terrifying it throbs; if it hears something
enraging it stops; if it is faced with death it
becomes sad; if it sees something beautiful it
is dazzled. But the heavenly heart in the head,
when would it have moved in the least? Dost
thou ask: Can the heavenly heart not move?
Then I answer: How can the true thought
in the square inch move! If it really moves,
that is not good. For when ordinary men die,
then it moves, but that is not good. It is best
indeed if the light has already solidified into
a spirit-body and its life-energy gradually
penetrated the instincts and movements. But
that is a secret which has not been revealed
for thousands of years.

The lower heart moves like a strong, powerful commander who despises the heavenly rule because of his weakness, and has
usurped the leadership in affairs of state. But
when the primal castle can be fortified and
defended, then it is as is a strong and wise
ruler sat upon the throne. The eyes start the
light circulating like two ministers at the
right and left who support the ruler with all
their might. When rule in the center is thus

in order, all those rebellious heroes will present themselves with lances reversed ready to take orders.

The way to the Elixir of Life knows as supreme magic, seed-water, spirit-fire, and thought-earth: these three. What is seed-water? It is the true, one energy of former heaven (eros). Spirit fire is the light (logos). Thought-earth is the heavenly heart of the middle dwelling (intuition). Spirit-fire is used for the foundation. Ordinary men make their bodies through thoughts. The body is not only the seven foot-tall outer body. In the body is the anima. The anima adheres to consciousness, in order to affect it. Consciousness depends for its origin on the anima. The anima is yin (feminine), it is the substance of consciousness. As long as this consciousness is not interrupted, it continues to beget from generation to generation, and the changes of form of the anima and the transformations of substance are unceasing.

But, besides this, there is the animus in which the spirit shelters. The animus lives in the daytime in the eyes; at night it houses in the liver. When living in the eyes, it sees; when housed in the liver, it dreams. Dreams are the wanderings of the spirit through all nine heavens and all nine earths. But whoever is in a dark and withdrawn mood on waking, and chained to his bodily form, is fettered by the anima. Therefore the concentration of the animus is brought about by the circulation of the light, and in this way the spirit is maintained, the anima subjugated, and consciousness cut off. The method used by the ancients for escaping from the world consisted in melting out completely the slag of darkness in order to return to the purely creative. This is nothing more than a reduction of the anima and a completion of the animus. And the circulation of the light is the magical means of reducing the dark, and gaining mastery over the anima. Even if the work is not directed towards bringing back the Creative, but confines itself to the magical means of the circulation of the light, it is just the light that is the Creative. By means of its circulation, one returns to the Creative. If this method is followed, plenty of seed-water will be present of itself; the spirit fire will be ignited, and the thought-earth will solidify and crystallize. And thus the holy fruit matures. The scarabaeus rolls his ball and in the ball there develops life as the result of the undivided effort of his spiritual concentration. If now an embryo can grow in manure, and shed its shells, why then should not the dwelling place of our heavenly heart also be able to create a body if we concentrate the spirit upon it?

The one effective, true human nature (logos united with vitality), when it descends into the house of the Creative, divides into animus and anima. The animus is I the heavenly heart. It is of the nature of light; it is the power of lightness and purity. It is that which we have received from the great emptiness, that which is identical in form with the primordial beginning. The anima partakes of the nature of the dark. It is the energy of the heavy and the turbid; it is bound to the bodily fleshly heart. The animus loves life. The anima seeks death. All sensuous desires and impulses of anger are effects of the anima; it is the conscious spirit which after death is nourished on blood, but which, during life, is in greatest distress. The dark returns to darkness and like things attract each other according to their kind. But the pupil understands how to distil the dark anima completely so that it transforms itself into pure light (yang).

[*** In this part there is described the role played by the primal spirit and the conscious spirit in the making of the human body. The Master says, The life of man is like that of a mayfly: only the true human nature of the primal spirit can transcend the cycle of heaven and earth and the fate of the aeons. The true human nature proceeds from that which has no polarity [the ultimate] whereby it takes the true essence of heaven and earth into itself and becomes the conscious spirit. As primal spirit it receives its human nature from father and mother. This primal spirit is without consciousness and knowledge, but is able to regulate the formative processes of the body. The conscious spirit is very evident and very effective, and can adapt itself unceasingly. It is the ruler of the human heart. As long as it stays in the body it is the animus. After its departure from the body it becomes spirit. While the body is entering into existence, the primal spirit has not yet formed an embryo in which it could incorporate itself. Thus it crystallizes itself in the non-polarized free One.

At the time of birth the conscious spirit inhales the energy and thus becomes the dwelling of the new-born. It lives in the heart. From that on the heart is master, and the primal spirit loses its place while the conscious spirit has the power.

The primal spirit loves stillness, and the conscious spirit loves movement. In its movement it remains bound to feelings and desires. Day and night it wastes the primal seed till the energy of the primal spirit is entirely used up. Then the conscious spirit leaves the shell and goes away.

Whoever has done good in the main has spirit-energy that is pure and clear when death comes. It passes out by the upper openings of mouth and nose. The pure and light energy rises upward and floats up to heaven and becomes the fivefold present shadow-genius, or shadow-spirit. But if, during life, the primal spirit was used by the conscious spirit for avarice, folly, desire, and lust, and committed all sorts of sins, then in the moment of death the spirit-energy is turbid and confused, and the conscious spirit passes out together with the breath, through the lower openings of the door of the belly. For if the spirit-energy is turbid and unclean, it crystallizes downward, sinks down to hell, and becomes a demon. Then not only does the primal spirit lose its nature, but the power and wisdom of true human nature is thereby lessened. Therefore the Master says, If it moves, that is not good.

If one wants to maintain the primal spirit one must, without fail, first subjugate the perceiving spirit. The way to subjugate it is through the circulation of the light. If one practices the circulation of the light, one must forget both body and heart. The heart must die, the spirit live. When the spirit lives, the breath will begin to circulate in a wonderful way. This is what the Master called the very best. Then the spirit must be allowed to dive down into the abdomen (solar plexus). The energy then has intercourse with spirit, and spirit unites with the energy and crystallizes itself. This is the method of starting the work.

In time, the primal spirit transforms itself in the dwelling of life into the true energy. At that time, the method of the turning of the millwheel must be applied, in order to distill it so that it becomes the Elixir of Life. That is the method of concentrated work.

When the Life Elixir pearl is finished, the holy embryo can be formed; then the work must be directed to the warming and nourishing of the spiritual embryo. That is the method of finishing.

When the energy-body of the child is fully formed, the work must be directed that the embryo is born and returns to emptiness. That is the method of ending the work.

From the most ancient times till today, this is not empty talk, but the sequence of the

Great Way in the true method of producing an eternally living and immortal spirit and holy man.

But if the work is so far consummated, then everything belonging to the dark principle is wholly absorbed, and the body is born into pure light. When the conscious spirit has been transformed into the primal spirit, then only one can say that it has attained an infinite capacity for transformations and, departing from the cycle of births, has been brought to the sixfold present, golden genius. If this method of ennobling is not applied, how will the way of being born and dying be escaped?]

Circulation of the Light and Protection of the Center

Master Lu-tsu said, since when has the expression "circulation of the ligh" been revealed? It was revealed by the "True Men of the Beginning of Form" (Kuan Yin-hsi). When the light is made to move in a circle, all the energies of heaven and earth, of the light and the dark, are crystallized. That is what is termed seed-like thinking, or purification of the energy, or purification of the idea. When one begins to apply this magic it is as if, in the middle of being, there were non-being. When in the course of time the work is completed, and beyond the body there is a body, it is as if, in the middle of non-being, there were being. Only after concentrated work of a hundred days will the light be genuine, then only will it become spirit-fire. After a hundred days there develops by itself in the midst of the light a point of the true light-pole (yang). Then suddenly there develops the seed pearl. It is as if man and woman embraced and a conception took place. Then one must be quite still and wait. The circulation of the light is the epoch of fire.

In the midst of primal transformation, the radiance of the light (yang-kuang), is the determining thing. In the physical world it is the sun; in man, the eye. The radiation and dissipation of spiritual consciousness is chiefly brought about by this energy when it is directed outward (flows downward). Therefore the Way of the Golden Flower depends wholly on the backward-flowing method.

[*** Man's heat stands under the fire trigram, Li. The flames of the fire press upward. When both eyes are looking at things of the world it is with vision directed outward. Now if one closes the eyes and, reversing the glance, directs it inward and looks at the room of the ancestors, that is the backward-flowing method. The energy of the kidneys is under the water sign. When the desires are stirred, it runs downward, is directed outward, and creates children. If, in the moment of release, it is not allowed to flow outward, but is led back by the energy of thought so that it penetrates the crucible of the Creative, and refreshes heart and body and nourishes them, that also is the backward-flowing method. Therefore it is said, The Way of the

Elixir of Life depends entirely on the backward-flowing method.]

The circulation of the light is not only a circulation of the seed-blossom of the individual body, but it is even a circulation of the true, creative, formative energies. It is not a momentary fantasy, but the exhaustion of the cycle (soul-migration) of all the aeons. Therefore the duration of a breath means a year according to human reckoning and a hundred years measured by the long night of the nine paths (of reincarnation).

After a man has the one sound of individuation (ho) behind him, he will be born outward according to the circumstances, and until his old age he will never look backward. The energy of the light exhausts itself and trickles away. That brings the ninefold darkness (of reincarnations) into the world. In the book Leng Yen it is said: "By concentrating the thoughts, one can fly; by concentrating the desires, one falls". When a pupil takes little care of his thoughts and much care of his desires, he gets into the path of submersion. Only through contemplation and quietness does true intuition arise: for that the backward-flowing method is necessary.

In the Book of the Secret Correspondences it is said: "Release is in the eye". In the Simple Questions of the Yellow Ruler it is said: "The seed-blossoms of the human body must be concentrated upward in the empty space". This refers to it. Immortality is contained in this sentence and also the overcoming of the world is contained in it. This is the common goal of all religions.

The light is not in the body alone, nor is it only outside the body. Mountains and rivers and the great earth are lit by sun and moon; all that is this light. Therefore it is not only within the body. Understanding and clarity, perception and enlightenment, and all movements (of the spirit) are likewise this light; therefore it is not just something outside the body. The light-flower of heaven and earth fills all the thousand spaces. But also the light-flower of the individual body passes through heaven and covers the earth. Therefore, as soon as the light is circulating, heaven and earth, mountains and rivers, are all circulating with it at the same time. To concentrate the seed-flower of the human body above the eyes, that is the great key of the human body. Children, take heed! If for a day you do not practice meditation, this light streams out, who knows whither? If you only meditate for a quarter of an hour, by it you can do away with a thousand births. All methods end in quietness. This marvelous magic cannot be fathomed.

But when the practice is started, one must press on from the obvious to the profound, from the coarse to the fine. Everything depends on there being no interruption. The beginning and the end of the practice must be one. In between there are cooler and warmer moments, that goes without saying. But the goal must be to reach the vastness of heaven and the depths of the sea, so that all methods seem quite easy and taken for granted. Only then have we mastered it.

All holy men have bequeathed this tone another: nothing is possible without con-templation (fang-chao, reflection). When Confucius says: "Perceiving brings one to the goal"; or when the Buddha calls it: "The vision of the heart"; or Lao-tse says: "Inner vision", it is all the same.

Anyone can talk about reflection, but he cannot master it if he does not know what the word means. What has to be reversed by reflection is the self-conscious heart, which has to direct itself towards that point where the formative spirit is not yet mani-fest. Within our six-foot body we must strive for the form which existed before the laying down of heaven and earth. If today people sit and meditate only one or two hours, looking only at their own egos, and call this reflection, how can anything come of it?

The two founders of Buddhism and Taoism have taught that one should look at the tip of one's nose. But they did not mean that one should fasten one's thoughts to the tip of the nose. Neither did they mean that, while the eyes were looking at the tip of the nose, the thoughts should be concentrated on the yellow middle. Wherever the eye looks, the heart is directed also. How can it be directed at the same time upward (yellow middle), and downward (tip of the nose), or alternatively, so that it is now up, now down? All that means confusing the finger which points to the moon with the moon itself.

What then is really meant by this? The expression "tip of the nose" is very cleverly chosen. The nose must serve the eyes as a guideline. If one is not guided by the nose, either one opens wide the eyes and looks into the distance, so that the nose is not seen, or the lids shut too much, so that the eyes close, and again the nose is not seen. But when the eyes are opened too wide, one makes the mistake of directing them outward, whereby one is easily distracted. If they are closed too much, one makes the mistake of letting them turn inward, whereby one easily sinks into a dreamy reverie. Only when the eyelids are lowered properly halfway is the tip of the nose seen in just the right way. Therefore it is taken as a guideline. The main thing is to lower the eyelids in the right way, and then to allow the light to streaming of itself; without effort, wanting the light to stream in concentratedly. Looking at the tip of the nose serves only as the beginning of the inner concentration, so that the eyes are brought into the right direction for looking, and then are held to the guideline: after that, one can let it be. That is the way a mason hangs up a plumb-line. As soon as he has hung it up, he guides his work by it without continually bothering himself to look at the plumb-line.

Fixating contemplation is a Buddhist method which has not by any means been handed down as a secret.

One looks with both eyes at the tip of the nose, sits upright and in a comfortable position, and holds the heart to the center in the midst of conditions. In Taoism it is called the yellow middle, in Buddhism the center of the midst of conditions. The two are the same. It is not necessarily mean the middle of the head. It is only a matter of fixing one's thinking on the point which lies exactly between two eyes. Then all is well. The light is something extremely mobile. When one fixes the thought on the mid-point between the two eyes, the light streams in of its own accord. It is not necessary to direct the attention especially to the middle castle. In these few words the most important thing is contained.

"The center in the midst of conditions" is a very subtle expression. The center is omnipresent; everything is contained in it; it is connected with the release of the whole process of creation. The condition is the portal. The condition, that is, the fulfillment of this condition, makes the beginning, but it does not bring about the rest with inevitable necessity. The meaning of these two words is very fluid and subtle.

Fixating contemplation is indispensable; it ensures the making fast of the enlightenment. Only one must not stay sitting rigidly if worldly thoughts come up, but one must examine where the thought is, where it began, and where it fades out. Nothing is gained by pushing reflection further. One must be content to see the thought arose, and not seek beyond the point of origin; for to find the heart (consciousness, to get behind consciousness with consciousness), that cannot be done. Together we want to bring the states of the heart to rest; that is true contemplation. What contradicts it is false contemplation. That leads to no goal. When the flight of the thoughts keeps extending further, one should stop and begin contemplating. Let one contemplate and then start fixating again. That is the double method of making fast the enlightenment. It means the circulation of the light. The circulation is fixation. The light is contemplation. Fixation without contemplation is circulation without light. Contemplation without fixation is light without circulation! Take note of that!

[*** The general meaning of this section is that protection of the center is important for the circulation of the light. The last section dealt with the theme that the human body is a very valuable possession when the primal spirit is master. But when it is used by the conscious spirit, the latter brings it about that, day and night, the primal spirit is scattered and wasted. When it is completely worn out, the body dies. Now the method is described whereby the conscious spirit can be subjected and the primal spirit protected; that is impossible if one does not begin by making the light circulate. It is like this: if a splendid is to be erected, a fine foundation must first be built. When the foundation is firm, then only can the work proceed and the base of the walls be deeply and solidly grounded, and the pillars and walls built up. If a foundation is not laid in this way, how can the house be completed? The method of cultivating life is exactly like that. The circulation of the light is to be compared with the foundation of the building. When the foundation stands firm, how quickly it can be built upon! To protect the yellow middle with the fire of the spirit, that is the work of building. Therefore the Master makes especially clear the method by which one enters into the cultivation of life, and bids people look with both eyes at the tip of the nose, to lower the lids, to look within, sit quietly with upright body, and fix the heart on the center in the midst of conditions.

Keeping the thoughts on the space between the two eyes allows the light to penetrate. Thereupon, the spirit crystallizes and enters the center in the midst of conditions. The center in the midst of conditions is the lower Elixir-field, the place of energy (solar plexus).

The Master hinted at this secretly when he said at the beginning of practice one must sit in a quiet room, the body like dry wood, the heart like cool ashes. Let the lids of both eyes be lowered; then look within and purify the heart, wash the thoughts, stop pleasures, and conserve the seed. Sit down daily to meditate with legs crossed. Let the light in the eyes be stopped; let the hearing power of the ear be crystallized and the tasting power of the tongue diminished; that is, the tongue shall be laid to the roof of the mouth; let the breathing through the nose be made rhythmical and the thoughts fixed on the dark door. If the breathing is not first made rhythmical it is to be feared that there will be difficulty in breathing, because of stoppage. When one closes the eyes, then one should take as a measure the point on the bridge of the nose which lies not quite half an inch below the intersection point of the line of vision, where there is a little bump on the nose. Then one begins to collect one's thought; the ears make the breathing rhythmical; body and heart are comfortable and harmonious. The light of the eyes must shine quietly, and, for a long time, neither sleepiness nor distraction must set in. The eyes do not look forward; they lower their lids and light up what is within. It shines on this place. The mouth does not speak nor laugh. One closes the lips and breathes inwardly. Breathing is at this place. The nose smells no odors. Smelling is at this place. The ear does not hear things outside. Hearing is at this place. The whole heart watches over what is within. Its' watching is at this place. The thoughts do not stray outward; true thoughts have duration in themselves. If the thoughts endure, the seed is enduring; if the seed endures, the energy endures; if the energy endures, then the spirit will endure. The spirit is thought; thought is the heart; the heart is the fire; the fire is the Elixir. When one looks at what is within in this way, the wonders of the opening and shutting of the gates of heaven will be inexhaustible. But the deeper secrets of the gates of heaven will be inexhaustible. But the deeper secrets cannot be effected without making the breathing rhythmical.

If the pupil begins and cannot hold his thoughts to the place between the two eyes; if he closes the eyes, but the energy o the heart does not enable him to view the space of energy, the cause is most probably that the breathing is too loud and hasty, and other evils arise from this, because body and heart are kept busy trying to suppress forcibly the uprush of energy and quick breath.

If the thoughts are held only to the two eyes, but the spirit is not crystallized in the solar plexus (the center in the midst of conditions), it is as if one had mounted to the hall but had not yet entered the inner chamber. Then the spirit-fire will not develop, the energy remains cold, and the true fruit will hardly manifest itself.

Therefore the Master harbors the fear lest, in their efforts, men only fix their thoughts on the pace on the nose, but fail to think of fixing their ideas on the space of energy; that is why he used the comparison of the mason with the plumb-line. The mason uses the plumb-line only in order to see if his wall is perpendicular or slanting, and for this the string serves as a guide-line. When he has determined the direction, he can begin the work. But then he works on the wall, not on the plumb-line. That is clear. From this it is seen that fixing the thoughts between the eyes means only what the plumb-line does to the mason. The Master refers again and again to this because he fears his meaning might not be understood. And even if the pupils have grasped the way of doing the thing, he fears they might interrupt their work, and so he says several times: "Only after a hundred days of consistent work, only then is the light genuine; only then can one begin work with the spirit-fire". If one proceeds in a collected fashion, after a hundred days there develops spontaneously in the light a point of the genuine creative light (yang). The pupils must examine that with sincere hearts.]

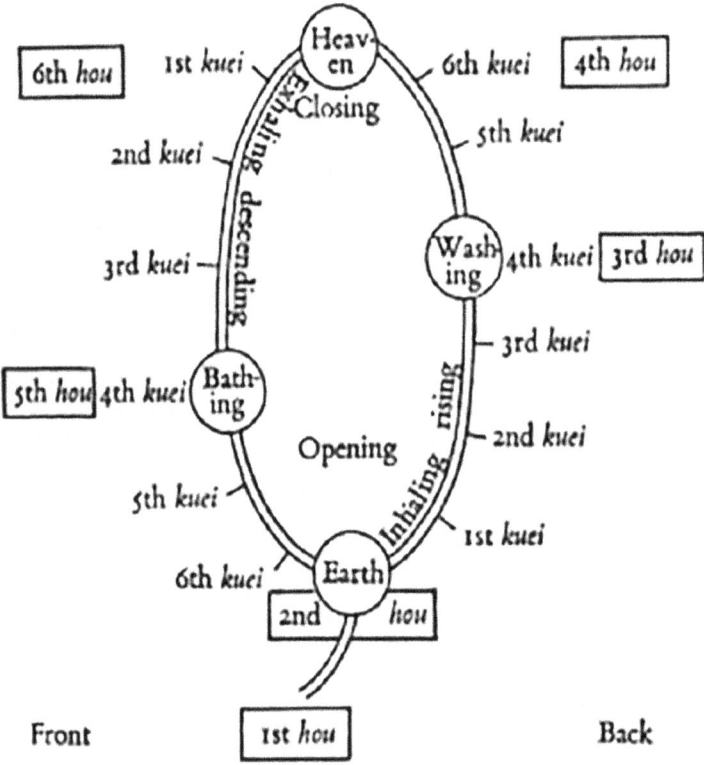

Heaven

Closing

6th hou | 1st *kuei* | 6th *kuei* | 4th hou

2nd *kuei*

5th *kuei*

Exhaling descending

3rd *kuei*

Wash-ing | 4th *kuei* | 3rd *hou*

3rd *kuei*

5th hou | 4th *kuei* | Bath-ing

Opening

2nd *kuei*

Inhaling rising

5th *kuei*

1st *kuei*

6th *kuei* | Earth

2nd | hou

Front

1st *hou*

Back

Circulation of the Light and Making the Breathing Rhythmical

Master Lu-tsu said, The decision must be carried out with a collected heart, and not seeking success; success will come of itself. In the first period of release there are chiefly two mistakes: indolence and distraction. But that can be remedied; the heart must not enter into the breathing too completely. Breathing comes from the heart. What comes out of the heart is breath. As soon as the heart stirs, there develops breath-energy. Breath-energy is originally transformed activity of the heart. When our ideas go very fast they imperceptibly pass into fantasies which are always accompanied by the drawing of a breath, because this inner and outer breathing hands together like tone and echo. Daily we draw innumerable breaths and have an equal number of fantasies. And thus the clarity of the spirit ebbs away as wood dries out and ashes die.

So, then, should a man have no imagining in his mind? One cannot be without imaginings. Should one not breathe? One cannot do without breathing. The best way is to make a medicine of the illness. Since heart and breath are mutually dependent, the circulation of the light must be united with the rhythm of breathing. For this, light of the ear is above all necessary. There is a light of the eye and a light of the ear. The light of the eye is the united light of the sun and moon outside. The light of the ear is the united seed of sun and moon within. The seed is thus the light in crystallized form. Both have the same origin and are different only in name. Therefore, understanding (ear) and clarity (eye) are one and the same effective light.

In sitting down, after lowering the lids, one uses the eyes to establish a plumb-line and then shifts the light downward. But if the transposition downward is not successful, then the heart is directed towards listening to the breathing. One should not be able to hear with the ear the outgoing and intaking of the breath. What one hears is that it has no tone. As soon as it has tone, the breathing is rough and superficial, and does not penetrate into the open. Then the heart must be made quite light and insignificant. The more it is released, the less it becomes; the less it is, the quieter. All at once it becomes so quiet that it stops. Then the true breathing is manifested and the form of the heart comes to consciousness. If the heart is light, the breathing is light, for every movement of the heart affects breath-energy. If breathing is light, the heart is light, for every movement of breath-energy affects the heart. In order to steady the heart, one begins by taking care of the breath-energy. The heart cannot be influenced directly. Therefore the breath-energy is sued as a handle, and this is what is called maintenance of the concentrated breath-energy.

Children, do you not understand the nature of movement? Movement can be produced by outside means. It is only another name for mastery. One can make the heart move merely by running. Should one not also be able to bring it to rest by concentrated quietness? The great holy ones who knew how the heart and breath-energy mutually influence one another have thought out an easier procedure in order to help posterity.

In the Book of the Elixir it is said: "The hen can hatch her eggs because her heart is always listening". That is an important magic spell. The hen can hatch the eggs because of the energy of heat. But the energy of the heat can only warm the shells; it cannot penetrate into the interior. Therefore she conducts this energy inward with her heart. This she does with her hearing. In this way she concentrates her whole heart. When the heart penetrates, the energy penetrates, and the chick receives the energy of the heat and begins to live. Therefore a hen, even when at times she leaves her eggs, always has the attitude of listening with bent ear. Thus the concentration of the spirit is not interrupted. Because the concentration of the spirit is not interrupted. But the concentration of the spirit suffers no interruption, neither does the energy of heat suffer interruption day or night, and the spirit awakens to life. The awakening of the spirit is accomplished because the heart has first died. When a man can let his heart die, then the primal spirit wakes to life. To kill the heart does not mean to let it dry and wither away, but it means that it has become undivided and gathered into one.

The Buddha said: "When you fix your heart on one point, then nothing is impossible for you". The heart easily runs away, so it is necessary to concentrate it by means of breath-energy. Breath-energy easily becomes rough, therefore it has to be refined by the heart. When that is done, can it then happen that it is not fixed?

The two mistakes of indolence and distraction must be combated by quiet work that is carried on daily without interruption; then success will certainly be achieved. If one is not seated in meditation, one will often be distracted without noticing it. To become conscious of the distraction is the mechanism by which to do away with distraction. Indolence of which a man is conscious, and indolence of which he is unconscious, are a thousand miles apart. Unconscious indolence is real indolence; conscious indolence is not complete indolence, because there is still some clarity in it. Distraction comes from letting the mind wander about; indolence comes from letting the mind wander about; indolence comes from the mind's not yet being pure. Distraction is much easier to correct than indolence. It is as in sickness: if one feels pains and irritations, one can help them with remedies, but indolence is like a disease that is attended by lack of realization. Distraction can be counteracted, confusion can be straightened out, but indolence and lethargy are heavy and dark. Distraction and confusion at least have a place, but in indolence and lethargy the anima alone is active. In distraction the animus is still present, but in indolence pure darkness rules. If one becomes sleepy during meditation, that is an effect of indolence. Only breathing serves to overcome indolence. Although the breath that flows in and out through the nose is not the true breath, the flowing in and out of the true breath takes place in connection with it.

While sitting, one must therefore always keep the heart quiet and the energy concentrated. How can the heart be made quiet? By the breath. Only the heart must be conscious of the flowing in and out of the breath; it must not be heard with the ears. If it is not heard, then the breathing is light; if light, it is pure. If it can be heard, then the breath-energy is rough; if rough, then it is troubled; if it is troubled, then indolence and lethargy develop and one wants to sleep. That is self-evident.

How to use the heart correctly during breathing must be understood. It is a use without use. One should only let the light fall quite gently on the hearing. This sentence contains a secret meaning. What does it mean to let the light fall? It is the spontaneous radiation of the light of the eyes. The eye looks inward only and not outward. To sense brightness without looking outward means to look inward. To sense brightness without looking outward means to look inward; it has nothing to do with an actual looking within. What does hearing mean? It is the spontaneous hearing of the light of the ear. The ear listens inwardly only and does not listen to what is outside. To sense brightness without listening to what is outside is to listen inwardly; it has nothing to do with actually listening to what is within. In this sort of hearing, one hears only that there is no sound; in this kind of seeing, one sees only that no shape is there. If the eye is not looking outward and the ear is not hearkening outward, they close themselves and are inclined to sink inward. Only when one looks and hearkens inward does the organ not go outward nor sink inward. In this way indolence and lethargy are done away with. That is the union of the seed and the light of the sun and moon.

If, as a result of indolence, one becomes sleepy, one should stand up and walk about. When the mind has become clear one should sit down again. If there is time in the morning, one may sit during the burning of an incense stick; that is the best. In the afternoon, human affairs interfere and one can therefore easily fall into indolence. It is not necessary, however, to have an incense stick. But one must lay aside all entanglements and

sit quite still for a time. In the course of time
there will be success without one's becoming
indolent and falling asleep.

[*** The chief thought of this section is
that the most important for achieving the circulation of the light is rhythmical breathing.
The further the work advances, the deeper
becomes the teaching. During the circulation of the light, the pupil must coordinate
heart and breathing in order to avoid the
annoyance of indolence and distraction. The
Master fears that when beginners have once
sat and lowered their lids, confused fantasies
may arise, because of which, the heart will
begin to beat so that it is difficult to guide.
Therefore he teaches the practice of count-
ing the breath and fixing the thoughts of the
heart in order to prevent the energy of the
spirit from flowing outward.

Because breath comes out of the heart,
unrhythmical breathing comes from the
heart's unrest. Therefore one must breathe
in and out quite softly so that it remains inau-
dible to the ear, and only the heart quietly
counts the breaths. When the heart forgets
the number of breaths, that is a sign that the
heart has gone off into the outer world. Then
one must hold the heart steadfast. If the ear
does not listen attentively, or the eyes do not

look at the bridge of the nose, it often happens that the heart runs off outside, or that sleep comes. That is a sign that the condition is going over into confusion and lethargy, and the seed-spirit must be brought into order again. If, in lowering the lids and taking direction from the nose, the mouth is not tightly closed and the teeth are not clenched firmly together, it can also easily happen that the heart hastens outwards; then one must close the mouth quickly and clench the teeth. The five senses order themselves according to the heart, and the spirit must have recourse to breath-energy so that heart and breath are harmonized. In this way there is need at most of daily work of a few quarter-hours for heart and breathing to come of themselves into the right sort of collaboration and harmony. Then one need no longer count and breathing becomes rhythmical of its own accord. When the breathing is rhythmical the mistakes of indolence and distraction disappear in time of their own accord.]

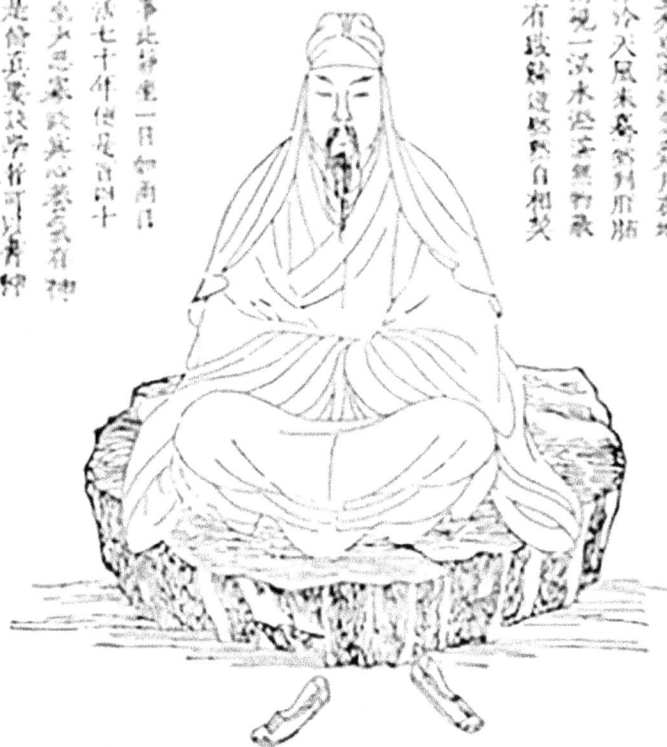

坐禪圖

臺大忘所細想莫見見月在地
冷冷入風未嘗斟料形骸
倚視一汎水浴空無行藏
串有玫婦連眼眼自相炙

經事此禪壹一目如两门
若濡七十件便是百四十
新宗多思家致爽心兼有神
此是偷安要故學行可以養神

Mistakes During the Circulation of the Light

Master Lu-tsu said, Your work will gradually become concentrated and mature, but before you reach the condition in which you sit like a withered tree before a cliff, there are still many possibilities of error which I would like to bring to your special attention. These conditions are recognized only when they have been personally experienced. I shall enumerate them here. Mt school differs from the Buddhist yoga school (Chan-tsung) in that it has confirmatory signs for each step of the way. First I would like to speak of the mistakes and then of the confirmatory signs.

When one begins to carry out one's decision, care must be taken so that everything can proceed in a comfortable, relaxed manner. Too much must not be demanded of the heart. One must be careful that, quite automatically, heart and energy are coordinated. Only then can a state of quietness be attained. During this quiet state the right conditions and the right space must be provided. One must not sit down [to meditate]

in the midst of frivolous. That is to say, the
mind must be free of vain preoccupations.
All entanglements must be put aside; one
must be detached and independent. Nor
must the thoughts be concentrated upon
the right procedure. This danger arises if
too much trouble is taken. I do not mean
that no trouble is to be taken, but the correct
way lies in keeping equal distance between
being and not being. If one can attain purposelessness through purpose, then the thing
has been grasped.. Now one can let oneself
go, detached and without confusion, in an
independent way.

Furthermore, one must not fall victim to
the ensnaring world. The ensnaring world is
where the five kinds of dark demons disport
themselves. This is the case, for example,
when, after fixation, one has chiefly thoughts
of dry wood and dead ashes, and few thoughts
of the bright spring on the great earth. In this
way one sinks into the world of the dark. The
energy is cold there, breathing is rough, and
many images of coldness and decay present themselves. If one tarries there long one
enters the world of plants and stones.

Nor must a man be led astray by the ten
thousand ensnarements. This happens if,
after the quiet state has begun, one after

another all sorts of ties suddenly appear. One wants to break through them and cannot; one follows them, and feels as if relieved by this. This means the master has become the servant. If a man tarries in this stage long he enters world of illusory desires.

At best, one finds oneself in heaven, at the worst, among the fox-sprits. Such a fox-spirit, it is true, may be able to roam in the famous mountains enjoying the wind and the moon, the flowers and fruits, and taking his pleasure in coral trees and jeweled grass. But after having done this for three to five hundred years, or at the most for a couple of thousand years, his reward is over and he is born again into the world of turmoil

All of these are wrong paths. When a man knows the wrong paths, he can then inquire into the confirmatory signs.

[*** The purpose of this section is to call attention to the wrong paths while meditating so that one enters the space of energy instead of that cave of fantasy. The latter is the world of demons. This, for example, is the case if one sits down to meditate and sees flames of light or bright colors appear, or if one sees Bodhisattvas and gods approach, or any other similar phantasms. Or, if one is not successful in uniting energy and breathing, if the water of the kidneys cannot rise, but presses downward, the primal energy becoming cold and breathing rough: then the gentle light-energies of the great earth are too few, and one lands in the gentle light-energies of the great earth are too few, and one lands in the empty fantasy-world. Or, when one has sat a long time, and ideas rise up in crowds and one tries to stop them, but cannot; one submits to being driven by them and feels easier: when this happens, one must get up and walk around a little until the heart and energy are again in unison; only then can one return to meditation. In meditating, a man must have a sort of conscious intuition, so that he feels energy and breathing unite in the field of the Elixir; he must feel that a warm release belonging to the true light is beginning to stir dimly. Then he has found the right space. When this right space has been found, one is freed from the danger of getting into the world of illusory desire or dark demons.]

Confirmatory Experiences During the Circulation of the Light

Master Lu-tsu said, There are many kinds of confirmatory experiences. One must not content oneself with small demands but must rise to the thought that all living creatures have to be redeemed. One must not be trivial and irresponsible in heart, but must strive to make deeds prove one's words.

If, when there is quiet, the spirit has continuously and uninterruptedly a sense of great joy as if intoxicated or freshly bathed, it is a sign that the light-principle is harmonious in the whole body; then the Golden Flower begins to bud. When, furthermore, all openings are quiet, and the silver moon stands in the middle of heaven, and one has the feeling that this great earth is a world of light and brightness, that is a sign that the body of the heart opens itself to clarity. It is a sign that the Golden Flower is opening.

Furthermore, the whole body feels strong and firm so that it fears neither storm not frost. Things by which other men are displeased, when I meet them, cannot becloud the brightness of the seed of the spirit. Yellow gold fills the house; the steps are of white jade. Rotten and stinking things on earth that come in contact with one breath of the true energy will immediately live again. Red blood becomes milk. The fragile body of the flesh is sheer gold and diamonds. That is a sign that the Golden Flower is crystallized.

The Book of Successful Contemplation (Ying-kuan-ching) says: "The sun sinks in the great water and magic pictures of trees in rows arise". The setting of the sun means that in chaos (in the world before phenomena, that is before the intelligible world) the foundation is laid: that is the non-polarized condition [ultimateless](wu-chi). Highest good is like water, pure and spotless. It is the ruler of the great polarity, the god who appears in the trigram of shock, Chen. Chen is also symbolized by wood, and soothe image of trees in rows appears. A sevenfold row of trees means the light of the seven body-openings (or heart-openings). The northwest is the direction of the Creative. When it moves on one place further, the Abysmal is there. The sun which sinks on one place further, the Abysmal is there. The sun which sinks into the great water is the image for the Creative and the Abysmal. The Abysmal is the direction of midnight (mouse, tzu, north). At the winter solstice, thunder (Chen) is in the middle of the earth quite hidden and covered up. Only when the trigram Chen is reached does the light-pole appear over the earth again. That is the image represented by the rows of trees. The rest can be correspondingly inferred.

The second part means the building of the foundation on this. The great world is like ice, a glassy jewel-world. The brilliancy of the light gradually crystallizes. Hence a great terrace arises and upon it, in the course o time, the Buddha appears. When the gold being appears who should it be but the Buddha? For the Buddha is the golden holy man of the great enlightenment. This is a great confirmatory experience.

Now there are three confirmatory experiences which can be tested. The first is that, when one has entered the state of meditation, the gods are in the valley. Men are heard talking as though at a distance of several hundred paces, each one quite clear. But the sounds are all like an echo in a valley. One can always hear them, but never oneself. This is called the presence of the gods in the valley.

At times the following can be experiences: as soon as one is quiet, the light of the eyes begins to blaze up, so that everything before

one becomes quite bright as if one were in a
cloud. If one opens one's eyes and seeks the
body, it is not to be found any more. This is
called: "In the empty chamber it grows light".
Inside and outside, everything is equally
light. That is a very favorable sign.

Or, when one sits in meditation, the fleshly
body becomes quite shining like silk or jade.
It seems difficult to remain sitting; one feels
as if drawn upward. This is called: "The spirit
returns and touches heaven". In time, one can
experience it in such a way that one really
floats upward.

And now, it is already possible to have all
three of these experiences. But not everything
can be expressed. Different things appear to
each person according to his dispositions. If
one experiences these things, it is a sign of
good aptitude. With these things it is just as
it is when one drinks water. One can tell for
oneself whether the water is warm or cold. In
the same way a man must convince himself
about these experiences, then only are they
real.

The Living Manner of the Circulation of the Light

Master Lu-tsu said, When there is a gradual success in producing the circulation of the light, a man must not give up his ordinary occupation in doing it. The ancients said, When occupations come to us, we must accept them; when things come to us, we must understand them from the ground up. If the occupations are properly handled by correct thoughts, the light is not scattered by outside things, but circulates according to its own law. Even the still invisible circulation of the light get started this way; how much more, then, is it the case with the true circulation of the light which has already manifested itself clearly.

When in ordinary life one has the ability always to react to things by reflexes only, without any admixture of a thought of others or of oneself, that is a circulation of the light arising out of circumstances. This is the first secret.

If, early in the morning, one can rid oneself of all entanglements and meditate from one to two double hours, and then can orientate oneself all activities and outside things in a purely objective, reflex way, and if this can be continued without any interruption, then after two or three months all the perfected ones come from heaven and approve such behavior.

[*** The receding section deals with the blissful fields that are entered when one goes forward in the work. The aim of this section is to show the pupils how they must shape their work more subtly day by day so that they may hope for an early attainment of the Elixir of Life. How does it happen that the master just at this point speaks to the fact that a man ought not to give up his ordinary way of life? It might be thought from this that the Master wanted to prevent the pupil from attaining the Elixir of Life quickly. He who knows replies to this, Not at all! The Master is concerned lest the pupil may not have fulfilled his karma, therefore he speaks in this way. Now if the work has already led into the blissful fields, the heart is like an expanse of water. When things come, it mirrors things; when things go, spirit and energy spontaneously unite again and do not allow themselves to be carried away by externals. That is what the Master means when he says that every entanglement in thought of other people and oneself must be completely given up. When the pupil succeeds in concentrating with true thoughts always on the space of energy, he does not have to start the light rotating, and the light rotates by itself. But when the light rotates, the Elixir is made spontaneously, and the performance of worldly tasks at the same time is not a hindrance. It is different at the beginning of the practice of meditation when spirit and energy are still scattered and confused. If worldly affairs cannot then be kept at a distance and a quiet place be found where one can concentrate with all one's energy, and thus avoid all disturbances from ordinary occupations, then one is perhaps industrious in the morning and certainly indolent in the evening. How long would it take till a man attained to the real secrets in this way? Therefore it is said, When on begins to apply oneself to the work, one should put aside household affairs. And, if that is not wholly possible, someone ought to be engaged to look after them so that one can take pains with complete attention. But when the work is so far advanced that secret confirmations are experienced, it does not matter if, at the same time, one's ordinary affairs are put in order, so that one can fulfill one's karma. This means the living manner of the circulation of the light. Long ago, the True Man of the Purple Polar Light (Tzu-yang chen-jen, or Chang Po-tuan) said: "If one cultivates one's action while mingling with the world and is still in harmony with the light, then the round is round and the angular has angles; then he lives among men, mysterious yet visible, different and yet the same, and none can compass it; then no one notices our secret actions". The living manner of the circulation of the light has jus this meaning: to live mingling with the world and yet in harmony with the light.]

A Magic Spell for the Far Journey

Master Lu-tsu said, Yu Ch'ing has left behind him a magic spell for the far journey:

Four words crystallize the spirit in the space of energy.

In the sixth month white snow is suddenly seen to fly.

At the third watch the sun's disk sends out blinding rays.

In the water blows the wind of the Gentle.

Wandering in heaven, one eats the spirit-energy of the Receptive.

And the still deeper secret of the secret:

The land that is nowhere, that is the true home...

These verses are full of mystery. The meaning is: The most important things in the great Tao are the words: action through non-action. Non-action prevents a man from becoming entangled in form and image (materiality). Action in non-action prevents a man from sinking into numbing emptiness and dead nothingness. The effect depends entirely on the central One; the releasing of the effect is in the two eyes. The two eyes are like the pole of the Great Wain which turns the whole of creation; they cause the poles of light and darkness to circulate. The Elixir depends from beginning to end on one thing: the metal in the midst of the water, that is, the lead in the water-region. Heretofore we have spoken of the circulation of the light, indicating thereby the initial release which works from without upon what lies within. This is to aid one in obtaining the Master. If is for pupils in the beginning stages. They go through the two lower transitions in order to gain the upper one. After the sequence of events is clear and the nature of the release is known, heaven no longer withholds the Way, but reveals the ultimate truth. Disciples, keep it secret and redouble your effort!

The circulation of the light is the inclusive term. The further the work advances, the more does the Golden Flower bloom. But there is a still more marvelous kind of circulation. Till now we have worked from the outside on what is within; now we stay in the center and rule what is external. Hitherto it was a service in aid of the Master; now it is a dissemination of the commands of the Master. The whole relationship is now reversed. If one wants to penetrate the more subtle regions by this method, one must first see to it that body and heart are completely controlled, that one is quite free and at peace, letting go of all entanglements, untroubled by the slightest excitement, and with the heavenly heart exactly in the middle. Then let one lower the lids of the two eyes as if one received a holy edict, a summons to come before the minister. Who would dare disobey? Then with both eyes one illumines the house of the Abysmal (water, K'an). Wherever the Golden Flower goes, the true light of polarity comes forth to meet it. The Clinging (brightness, Li) is bright outside and dark within; this is the body of the Creative. The one dark [line] enters and becomes master. The result is that the heart (consciousness) develops in dependence on things, is directed outward, and is tossed about on the stream. When the rotating light shines towards what is within, it does not develop in dependence on things, the energy of the dark is fixed, and the Golden Flower shines concentratedly. This is then the collected light of polarity. Related things attract each other. Thus the polarized light-line of the Abysmal presses upward. It is not only the light in the abyss, but it is creative light which meets creative light. As soon as these two substances meet each other, they unite inseparably, and there develops an unceasing life; it comes and goes, rises and falls of itself, in the house of the primal energy. One is aware of effulgence and infinity. The whole body feels light and would like to fly. This is the state of which it is said: Clouds fill the thousand mountains. Gradually it goes to and fro quite softly; it rises and falls imperceptibly. The pulse stands still and breathing stops. This is the moment of true creative union, the state of which it is said: The moon gathers up the ten thousand waters. In the midst of this darkness, the heavenly heart suddenly begins a movement. This is the return of the one light, the time when the child comes to life.

However, the details of this must be carefully explained. When a person looks at something, listens to something, eyes and ears move and follow the things until they have passed. These movements are all underlings, and when the heavenly ruler follows them in their task it means: to live together with demons.

If now, during every movement of rest, a person lives together with people and not with demons, then the heavenly ruler is the true man. When he moves, and we move with him, then the movement is the root of heaven. When he is quiet, and we are quiet with him, then this quietness is the cave of the moon. When he unceasingly alternates movement and rest, go on with him unceasingly in movement and quietness. When he rises and falls with inhaling and exhaling, rise and fall with him. That is what is called going to and fro between the root of heaven and the cave of the moon.

When the heavenly heart still preserves calm, movement before the right time is a fault of softness. When the heavenly heart has already moved, the movement that follows afterwards, in order to correspond with it, is a fault of rigidity. As soon as the heavenly heart is stirring, one must immediately mount upward whole-heartedly to the house of the Creative. Thus the spirit-light sees the summit; this is the leader. This movement is in accord with the time. The heavenly heart rises to the summit of the Creative, where it expands in complete freedom. Then suddenly it demands the deepest silence, and one must lead it speedily and whole-heartedly into the yellow castle; thus the eyes behold the central yellow dwelling place of the spirit.

When the desire for silence comes, not

a single thought arises; he who is looking inward suddenly forgets that he is looking. At this time, body and heart must be left completely released. All entanglements have disappeared without trace. Then I no longer know at what place the house of my spirit and my crucible are. If a man wants to make certain of his body, he cannot get at it. This condition is the penetration of heaven into earth, the time when all wonders return to their roots. So it is when the crystallized spirit goes into the space of energy.

The One is the circulation of the light. When one begins, it is at first still scattered and one wants to collect it; the six senses are not active. This is the cultivation and nourishment of one's own origin, the filling up of the oil when one goes to receive life. When one is far enough to have gathered it, one feels light and free and need not take the least trouble. This is the quieting of the spirit in the space of the ancestors, the taking possession of former heaven.

When one is so far advanced that every shadow and every echo has disappeared, so that one is entirely quiet and firm, this is refuge within the cave of energy, where all that is miraculous returns to its roots. One does not alter the place, but the place divides itself. This is incorporeal space where a thousand and ten thousand places are one place. One does not alter the time, but the time divides itself. This is immeasurable time when all the aeons are like a moment.

As long as the heart has not attained absolute tranquility, it cannot move itself. One moves the movement and forgets the movement; this is not movement in itself. Therefore it is said: If, when stimulated by external things, one moves, it is the impulse of the being. If, when not stimulated by external things, one moves, it is the movement of heaven. The being that is placed over against heaven can fall and come under the domination of the impulses. The impulses are based upon the fact that there are external things. They are thoughts that goon beyond one's own position. Then movement leads to movement. But when no idea arises, the right ideas come. That is the true idea. When things are quiet and one is quite firm, and the release of heaven suddenly moves, is this not a movement without purpose? Action through non-action has just this meaning.

As to the poem at the beginning, the two first lines refer entirely to the activity of the Golden Flower. The two next lines are concerned with the mutual interpenetration of sun and moon. The sixth month is the Cling-ing (Li, fire). The white snow that flies is the true polar darkness in the middle of the fire trigram, that is about to turn into the Recep-tive. The third watch is the Abysmal (K'an, water). The sun's disk is the one polar line in te trigram for water, which is about to turn into the Creative. This contains the way to take the trigram for the Abysmal and the way to reverse the trigram for the Clinging (fire, Li).

The following two lines have to do with the activity of the pole of the Great Wain, the rise and fall of the whole release of polarity. Water is the trigram of the Abysmal; the eye is the wind of the Gentle (Sun). The light of the eyes illumines the house of the Abysmal, and controls there the seed of the great light. "In heaven" means the house of the Creative (Ch'ien). "Wandering in heaven, one eats the spirit-energy of the Receptive". This shows how the spirit penetrates the energy, how heaven penetrates the earth; this happens so that the fire can be nourished.

Finally, the two last lines point to the deep-est secret, which cannot be dispensed with from the beginning to the end. This is the washing of the heart and the purification of the thoughts; this is the bath. The holy science takes as a beginning the knowledge of where to stop, and as an end, stopping at the highest good. Its beginning is beyond polarity.

The Buddha speaks of the transient, the creator of consciousness, as being the fundamental truth of religion. And the whole work of completing life and human nature in our Taoism lies in the expression "to bring about emptiness". All three religions agree in the one proposition, the finding of the spiritual Elixir in order to pass from death to life. In what does this spiritual Elixir consist? It means forever dwelling in purposelessness. The deepest secret of the bath that is to be found in our teaching is thus confined to the work of making the heart empty. Therewith the matter is settled. What I have revealed here in a word is the fruit of a decade of effort.

If you are not yet clear as to how far all three sections can be present in one section, I will make it clear to you through the threefold Buddhist contemplation of emptiness, delusion, and the center.

Emptiness comes as the first of the three contemplations. All things are looked upon as empty. Then follows delusion. Although it is known that they are empty, things are not destroyed, but one attends to one's affairs in the midst of the emptiness. But though one does not destroy things, neither does one pay attention to them; this is contemplation of the center. While practicing contemplation of the empty, one also knows that one cannot destroy the ten thousand things, and still one does not notice them. In this way the three contemplations fall together. But after all, strength is in envisioning the empty. Therefore, when one practices contemplation of emptiness, emptiness is certainly empty, but delusion is empty too. Being on the way of the center, one also creates images of the emptiness; they are not called empty, but are called central. One practices also contemplation of delusion, but one does not call it delusion, one calls it central. As to what has to do with the center, more need not be said.

[*** This section mentions first Yu Ch'ing's magical spell for the far journey. This magical spell states that the secret wonder of the Way is how something develops out of nothing. In that spirit and energy unite in crystallized form, there appears, in the course of time, in the midst of the emptiness of nothing, a point of true fire. During this time the more quiet the spirit becomes, the brighter is the fire. The brightness of the fire is compared with the sun's heat in the sixth month. Because the blazing fore causes the water of the Abysmal to vaporize, the steam is heated, and when it has passed the boiling point it mounts upward like flying snow. It is meant by this that one may see snow fly in the sixth month. But because the water is vaporized by the fire, the true energy is awakened; yet when the dark is at rest, the true energy is awakened; yet when the dark is at rest, the light begins to move; it is like the state of midnight. Therefore adepts call this time the time of the living midnight. At this time one works at the energy with the purpose of making it flow backward and rise, and flows down to fall like the upward spinning of the sun-wheel. Therefore it is said: "At the third watch the sun's disk sends out blinding rays". The rotation method makes use of breathing to blow in the fire of the gates of life; in this way one succeeds in bringing to blow on the fire of the gates of life; in this way one succeeds in bringing the true energy to its original place. Therefore it is said that the wind blows in the water. Out of the single energy of former heaven, there develops the out- and in-going breath of later heaven and its inflaming energy.

The way leads from the sacrum upward

in a backward-flowing way to the summit of the Creative, and on through the house of the Creative; then it sinks through the two stories in a direct downward-flowing way into the solar plexus, and warms it. Therefore it is said: "Wandering in heaven, one eats the spirit-energy of the Receptive". Because the true energy goes back into the empty place, in time, energy and form become rich and full, body and heart become glad and cheerful. If, by the practice of the turning of the wheel of the doctrine, this cannot be achieved, how otherwise should one be able to enter upon this far journey? What it amounts to is this: the crystallized spirit radiates back to the spirit-fire and, by means of the greatest quiet, fans the "fire in the midst of the water", which is in the middle of the empty cave. Therefore it is said: "And the still deeper secret of the secret: the land that is nowhere, that is the true home".

The pupil has already penetrated in his work into mysterious territory; but if he does not know the method of melting, it is to be feared that the Elixir of Life will hardly be produced. Therefore the Master has revealed the secret strictly guarded by the former holy men. When the pupil keeps the crystallized spirit fixed within the cave of energy and, at the same time, lets greatest quietness hold sway, then out of the obscure darkness a something develops from the nothingness, that is, the Golden Flower of the great One appears. At this time the conscious light is differentiated from the light of human nature [hsing]. Therefore it is said: "To move when stimulated by external things leads to its going directly outward and creating a man, that is the conscious light". If, at the time the true energy has been sufficiently collected, the pupil does not let it flow directly outward, but makes it flow backward, that is the light of life; the method of turning of the water-wheel must be applied. If one continues to turn, the true energy returns to the roots, drop by drop. Then the water-wheel stops, the body is clean, the energy is fresh. One single turning means one heavenly cycle, what Master Ch'iu has called a small heavenly cycle. If one does not wait to use the energy until it has been collected sufficiently, it is then too tender and weak, and the Elixir is not formed. If the energy is there and not used, then it becomes too old and rigid, and then, too, the Elixir of Life will hardly be produced. When it is neither too old nor too tender, then is the right time to use it purposefully. This is what the Buddha means when he says: "The phenomenon flows into emptiness". This is the sublimation of the seed into energy. If the pupil does not understand this principle, and lets the energy flow out directly, then the energy changes into seed; this is what is meant when it is said: "Emptiness finally flows into phenomena". But every man who unites bodily with a woman feels pleasure first and then bitterness; when the seed has flowed out, the body is tired and the spirit weary. It is quite different when the adept lets spirit and energy unite. That brings first purity and then freshness; when the seed is transformed, the body is healthy and free. There is a tradition that the old master P'eng grew to be 800 years old because he made use of serving maids to nourish his life, but that is a misunderstanding. In reality, he used the method of sublimation of spirit and energy. In the Elixir of Life symbols are used for the most part, and in them the fire of the Cling-ing (Li) is frequently compared to a bride, and the water of the Abyss to the boy (puer aeternus). From this arose the misunder-standing about Master P'eng having restored his virility through women. These are errors that have forced their way in later.

But adepts can use the means of over-throwing the Abysmal (K'an) and the Clinging (Li) only when they have sincere intention in the work, otherwise a pure mixture cannot be produced. The true purpose is subject to the earth; the color of the earth is yellow, therefore in books on the Elixir of Life it is symbolized by the yellow germ. When the Abysmal and the Clinging (Li) unite, the Golden Flower appears; the golden color is white, and therefore white snow is used as a symbol. But worldly people who do not understand the secret words of the Book of the Elixir of Life have misunderstood ad the yellow and white there in that they have taken it as a means of making gold out of stones. Is not that foolish?

An ancient adept said: "Formerly, every school knew this jewel, only fools did not know it wholly". If we reflect on this we see that the ancients really attained long life by the help of the seed-energy present in their own bodies, and did not lengthen their years by swallowing this or that sort of elixir. But the worldly people lost the roots and clung to the tree-tops. The Book of the Elixiralso says: "When the right man (white magician) makes use of the wrong means, the wrong means work in the right way". By this is meant the transformation of seed into energy. "But if the wrong man uses the right means, the right means work in the wrong way". By this is meant the bodily union of man and woman fro which spring sons and daughters. The fool wastes the most precious jewel of his body in energy. When it is finished, the boy perishes. The holy and wise men have no other way of cultivating their lives except by destroying lusts and safeguarding the seed. The accumulated seed is transformed into energy, and the energy, when there is enough of it, makes the creatively strong body. The difference shown by ordinary people depends only upon how they apply the downward-flowing way or the backward-flowing way.

The whole meaning of this section is directed towards making clear to the pupil the method of filling up the oil when meeting life. Here the eyes are the chief thing. The two eyes are the handle of the pole star. Even as heaven turns about the polar star as a center point, so among men the right intention must be the master. Therefore the completion of the Elixir of Life depends entirely on the harmonizing of the right purpose. Then, if it is said that the foundation can be laid in a hundred days, first of all the degree of industry in work and the degree of strength in the physical constitution must be taken into account. Whoever is eager in the work, and has a strong constitution, succeeds more quickly in turning the water-wheel of the rear river. When a person has found the method of making thoughts and energy harmonize with one another, he can complete the Elixir within the hundred days. But whoever is weak and inert will not produce it even after the hundred days. When the Elixir is completed, spirit and energy are pure and clear; the heart is empty, human nature (hsing) manifest, and the light of consciousness transforms itself into the light of human nature, the Abysmal and the Clinging (fire, Li) have intercourse spontaneously. When the Abysmal and the Clinging commingle, the holy fruit is born. The ripening of the holy fruit is the effect of a great heavenly cycle. Further elucidation stops with the method of the heavenly cycle.

This book is concerned with the means of cultivating life and shows at first how to start by looking at the bridge of one's nose; here the method of reversing is shown; the methods of making firm and letting go are in another book, the Hsu Ming Fang (Methods of Prolonging Life).]

Summary of the Chinese Concepts on Which is Based the Idea of the Golden Flower, or Immortal Spirit-Body

The Tao, the undivided, great One, gives

rise to two opposite reality principles, the dark and the light, yin and yang. These are at first thought of only as forces of nature apart from man,. Later, the sexual polarities and others as well are derived from them. From yin comes K'un, the receptive feminine principle; from yin come Ch'ien, the creative masculine principle; from yin comes ming, life; from yang, hsing or human nature.

Each individual contains a central monad, which, at the moment of conception, splits into life and human nature, ming and hsing. These two are supra-individual principles, and so can be related to eros and logos.

In the personal bodily existence of the individual they are represented by two other polarities, a p'o soul (or anima) and a hun soul (animus). All during the life of the individual these two are in conflict, each striving for mastery. At death they separate and go different ways. The anima sinks to earth as kuei, a ghost-being. The anima rises and becomes shen, a spirit or god, Shen may in time return to the Tao.

If the life-energy flows downward, that is, without let or hindrance into the outer world, the anima is victorious over the animus; no spirit-body or Golden Flower is developed, and at death the ego is lost. If the life-energy

is led through the backward-flowing process, that is, conserved, and made to rise
instead of allowed to dissipate, the animus
has been victorious, and the ego persists
after death. It then becomes shen, a spirit or
god. A man who holds to the way of conser-
vation all through life may reach the stage
of the Golden Flower, which then frees the
ego from the conflict of the opposites, and it
again becomes part of the Tao, the undivided,
great One.

踵蒂吸呼圖

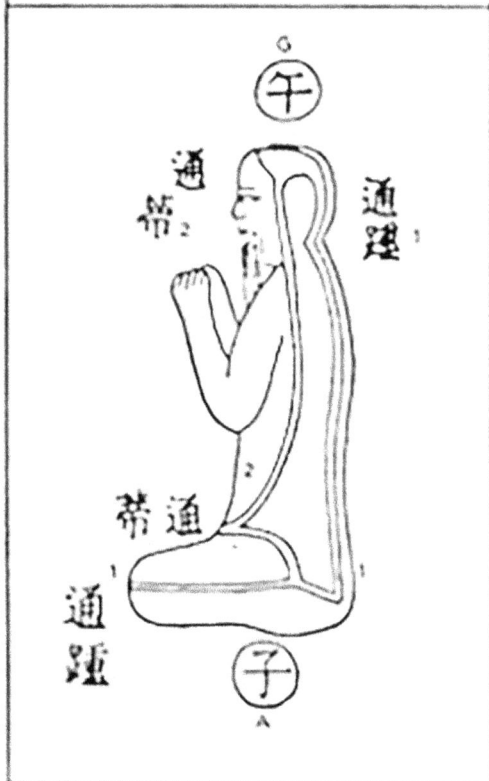

午

通
蒂

通
踵

蒂通

通
踵

子

THE HUI MING CHING

THE BOOK OF CONSCIOUSNESS AND LIFE
(Translation and Commentary by Richard Wilhelm)

此時丹熟更須慈母惜嬰兒

炁穴法名無盡藏
歲歲秋蘩蘩包容
我聞室中誰氏子
他云是你主人翁

行住坐卧
龍蛇守護
綿綿若存
念念在茲

去饑喘之患
孕蛾蛉之子
傳低揚之氣兼
溫濕其氣機
其氤隨其火
小蛾得其真

滑蓮今已化飛龍
聖見神运不可窮
一朝跳出諸光外
淨身真到紫微官

長養靈胎
內外無虧
沉瀘根深
神水常流

他日雲飛方見真人朝上帝

Cessation of Outflowing

If thou wouldst complete the diamond body
with no outflowing,

Diligently heat he roots of consciousness
and life.

Kindle light in the blessed country ever
close at hand,

And there hidden, let thy true self always
dwell.

[The illustration found here in the Chinese text shows the body of a man. In the middle of the lower half of the body is drawn a germ cell by which the gateway of life is separated from the gateway of consciousness. In between, leading to the outside world, is the canal through which the vital fluids flow out.]

The subtlest secret of the Tao is human nature and life (hsing-ming). There is no better way of cultivating human nature and life than to bring both back to unity. The holy men o ancient times, and the great sages, set forth their thoughts about the unification of human nature and life by means of images from the external world.; they were reluctant to speak of it openly without allegories. Therefore the secret of how to cultivate both simultaneously was lost one earth. What I show through a series of images is not a frivolous giving away of secrets. On the contrary, because I combined the notes of the Leng-yen-ching on the cessation of outflowing and the secret thoughts of Hua-yen-ching with occasional references to the other sutras, in order to summarize them in this true picture, it can be understood that consciousness and life are not anything external to the germinal vesicle. I have drawn this picture so that companions pursuing the divine workings of the dual cultivation may know that in this way the true seed matures, that in this way the cessation of outflowing is brought about, that in this way the sheli [Satira, the firm, the immortal body] is melted out, that in this way the great Tao is completed.

But the germinal vesicle is an invisible cavern; it has neither form nor image. When the vital breath stirs, the seed of this vesicle comes into being; when it cease it disappears again. It is the pace which harbors truth, the altar upon which consciousness and life are made. It is called the dragon castle at the bottom of the sea, the boundary region of the snow mountains, the primordial pass, the kingdom of greatest joy, the boundless country. All these different names mean this germinal vesicle. If a dying man does not know this germinal vesicle, he will not find the unity of consciousness and life in a thousand births, nor in ten thousand aeons.

This germinal point is something great. Before this our body is born of our parents, at the time of conception, this seed is first created and human nature and life dwell therein. The two are intermingled and form a unity, inseparably mixed like the sparks in the refining furnace, a combination of primordial harmony and divine law. Therefore it is said: "In the state before the appearance there is an inexhaustible breath". Furthermore it is said: "Before the parents have begotten the child, the breath of life is complete and the embryo perfect". But when the embryo moves and the embryo vesicle is torn, it is as if a man lost his footing on a high mountain: with a cry the man plunges down to earth, and from then on human nature and life are divided. From this moment human nature can no longer see life nor life human nature. And now date takes its course: youth passes over into maturity, maturity into old age, and old age into woe.

Therefore the Julia (Buddha Tathagata), in his great compassion, let the secret making and melting be known. He teaches one to re-enter the womb and create anew the human nature and life of the ego; he shows how spirit and soul (vital breath) enter the germinal vesicle, how they must combine to become a unity in order to complete the true fruit, just as the sperm and soul of father and mother entered into this germinal vesicle and united as one being in order to complete the embryo. The principle is the same.

Within the germinal vesicle is the fire of the ruler; at the entrance of the germinal vesicle is the fire of the minister; in the whole body, the fire of the people. When the fire of the ruler expresses itself, it is received by the fire of the minister. When the fire of the minister moves, the fire of the people follows him. When the three fires express themselves in this order a man develops. But when the three fires return in reverse order the Tao develops.

This is the reason that all the sages began their work at the germinal vesicle in which outflowing had ceased. If one does not establish this path, but sets up other things, it is of no avail. Therefore all the schools and sects which do not know that the ruling principle of consciousness and life is in this germinal vesicle, and which therefore seek it in the outer world, can accomplish nothing despite all their efforts to find it outside.

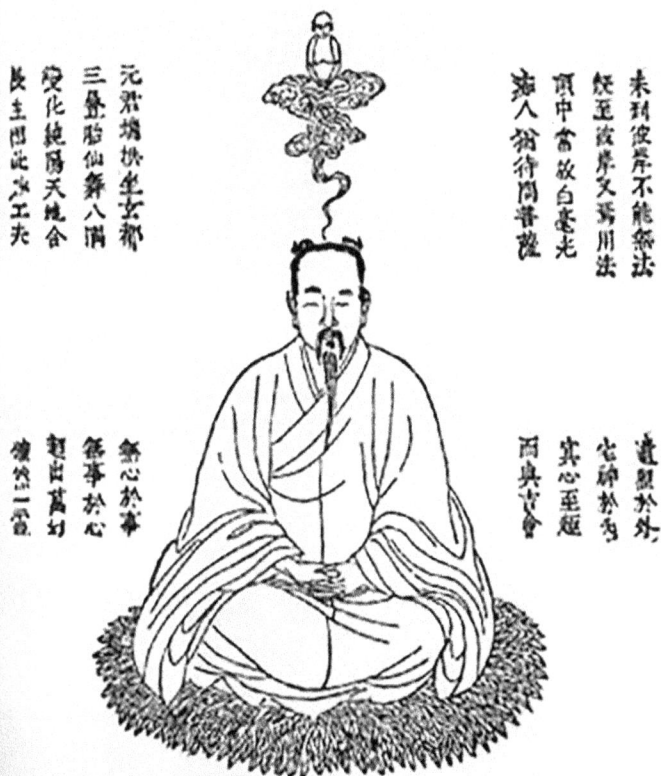

Meditation, Stage 3: Separation of the spirit-body for independent existence.

出胎圖

The Six Periods of Circulation in Conformity with the Law

If one discerns the beginning of the Buddha's path,

There will be the blessed city of the West.

After the circulation in conformity with the law,

There is a turn upward towards heaven when the breath is drawn in.

When the breath flows out energy is directed towards the earth.

One time-period consists of six intervals (hou).

In two intervals one gathers Moni (Sakyamuni).

The great Tao comes forth from the center.

Do not seek the primordial seed outside!

The most marvelous effect of the Tao is the circulation in conformity with the law. What makes the movement inexhaustible is the path. What best regulates the speed are the rhythms (kuei). What best determines the number of the exercises is the method of the intervals (hou).

This presentation contains the whole law, and the true features of the Buddha from the West are contained in it. The secrets contained in it show how one gets control o the process by exhaling and inhaling, how the alternation between decrease and increase expresses itself in closing and opening, how one needs true thoughts in order not to deviate from the way, how the firm delimitation of the regions makes it possible to begin and to stop at the right time.

I sacrifice myself and serve man, because I have presented fully this picture which reveals the heavenly seed completely, so that every layman and man of the world can reach it and so bring it to completion. He who lacks the right virtue may well find something in it, but heaven will not grant him his Tao. Why not? The right virtue belongs to the Tao as does one wing of a bird to the other: if one is lacking, the other is of no use. Therefore there is needed loyalty and reverence, humaneness and justice and strict adherence to the five commandments [of Buddhism: Do not kill, steal, commit adultery, lie, nor drink alcohol nor eat meat]; then only does one have the prospect of attaining something.

But all the subtleties and secrets are offered

in this Book of Consciousness and Life to be pondered and weighted, so that one can attain everything in its truth.

[*** The drawing is intended to show the circulation of the streams of energy during the movement of breathing. Inhalation is accompanied by the sinking of the abdomen and exhalation by the lifting of it, but in these exercises the point is that we have a backward-flowing movement as follows: when inhaling, one opens the lower energy-gate and allows the energy to rise upward along the rear line of energy (in the spinal cord), and this upward flow corresponds to the time-intervals indicated in the drawing. In exhaling, the upper gate is closed and the stream of energy is allowed to flow downward along the front line, likewise in the order of the time-intervals indicated. Furthermore, it is to be noted that the stations for "washing" and "bathing" do not lie exactly in the middle of the lines, but that "washing" is somewhat above and "bathing" somewhat below the middle, as the drawing shows.]

The Two Energy-Paths of Function and Control

There appears the way of the in-breathing and out-breathing of the primordial pass.

Do not forget the white path below the circulation in conformity wit the law!

Always let the cave of eternal life be nourished through the fire!

Ah! Test the immortal place of the gleaming pearl!

[*** In the text there is another picture here which is very similar to the first. It shows again the paths of energy: the one in front leads down and is called the function-path (jen), and the one at the back leading upwards is the control-path (tu).]

This picture is really the same as the one that precedes it. The reason that I show it again is so that the person striving for cultivation of the Tao may know that there is in his own body a circulation with the law. I have furnished this picture in order to enlighten companions in search of the goal. When these two paths (the functioning and

the controlling) can be brought into unbro-
ken connection, then all energy-paths are
joined. The deer sleeps with his nose on his
tail in order to close his controlling energy-
path. The crane and the tortoise close their
functioning-paths. Hence these three ani-
mals become at least a thousand years old.
How much further can a man go! A man who
carries on the cultivation of the Tao, who sets
in motion the circulation in conformity with
the law, in order to let consciousness and life
circulate, need not fear that he is not length-
ening his life and is not completing his path.

According to the law, but without exertion,
one must diligently fill oneself with light.
Forgetting appearance, look within and
help the true spiritual power!
Ten months them embryo is under fire.
After a year the washing and baths become
warm.

This picture will be found in the original edition of the Leng-yen-ching. But the
ignorant monks who did not recognize the
hidden meaning and knew nothing about
the embryo of the Tao have for this reason
made the mistake of leaving this picture out.
I only found out through the explanations of

adepts that the Julai (Tathagata) knows real work on the embryo of the Tao. This embryo is nothing corporeally visible which might be completed by other beings, but is in reality the spiritual breath-energy of the ego. First the spirit must penetrate the breath-energy (the soul), then the breath-energy envelops the spirit. When spirit and breath-energy are firmly united and the thoughts quiet and immobile, this is described as the embryo. The breath-energy must crystallize; only then will the spirit become effective. Therefore it is said in the Leng-yen-ching: "Take maternal care of the awakening and the answering". The two energies nourish and strengthen one another. Therefore it is said: "Daily growth takes place". When the energy is strong enough and the embryo is round and complete it comes out on the top of the head. This is what is called: the completed appearance which comes forth as embryo and begets itself as the son of the Buddha.

The Birth of the Fruit

Outside the body there is a body called the Buddha image.

The thought which is powerful, the absence of thoughts, is Bodhi.

The thousand-petal lotus flower opens, transformed through breath-energy.

Because of the crystallization of the spirit, a hundred-fold splendor shines forth.

圖 胎 道

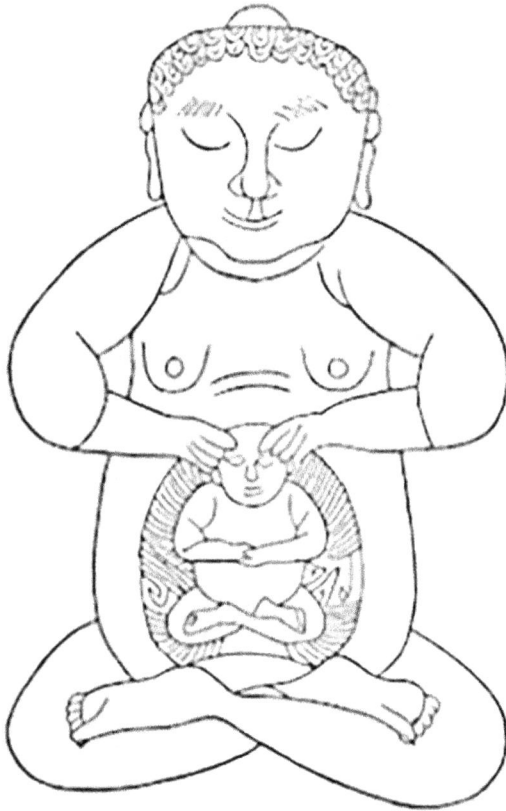

圖 形 現 兒 嬰

Fig-6. The Embryo of the Tao

In the Leng-yen-chou [Suramgama mantra] it is said: "At that time the ruler of the world caused a hundredfold precious light to beam from his hair knots. In the midst of the light shone the thousand-petal, precious lotus flower. And there within the flower sat a transformed Julai. And from the top of his head went ten rays of white, precious light, which were visible everywhere. The crowd looked up to the outstreaming light and the Julai announced: 'The divine, magic mantra is the appearance of the light-spirit, therefore his name is Son of Buddha'".

If a man does not receive the teaching about consciousness and life, how could there develop out of his own body the Julai, who sits and shines forth in the lotus flower and appears in his own spirit-body! Many say that the light-spirit is a minor teaching; but how can that which a man receives from the ruler of the world be a minor teaching? Herewith I have betrayed the deepest secret of the Leng-yen in order to teach disciples. He who receives this way rises at once to the dark secret and no longer becomes submerged in the dust of everyday life.

Concerning the Retention of the

Transformed Body

Every separate thought takes shape and becomes visible in color and form. The total spiritual power unfolds its traces and transforms itself into emptiness. Going out into being and going into non-being, one completes the miraculous Tao. All separate shapes appear as bodies, united with a true source.

The Face Turned to the Wall

The shapes formed by the spirit-fire are only empty colors and forms.

The light of human nature [hsing] shines back on the primordial, the true.

The imprint of the heart floats in space; untarnished, the moonlight shines.

The boat of life has reached the shore; bright shines the sunlight.

Empty Infinity

Without beginning, without end, Without past, without future.

A halo of light surrounds the world of the law.

We forget one another, quiet and pure, altogether powerful and empty. The emptiness is irradiated by the light of the heart and of heaven. The water of the sea is smooth and mirrors the on in its surface. The clouds disappear in blue space; the mountains shine clear. Consciousness reverts to contemplation; the moon disk rests alone.

www.ingramcontent.com/pod-product-compliance
Lightning Source LLC
Chambersburg PA
CBHW071406160426
42813CB00084B/591

*9 7 8 1 9 5 7 9 9 0 1 2 5 *